Truant Pastures

Truant Pastures

The Complete Poems of Harry C. Staley

Harry C. Staley

excelsior editions
State University of New York Press
Albany, New York

Published by State University of New York Press, Albany

For information, contact State University of New York Press, Albany, NY
www.sunypress.edu

Excelsior Editions is an imprint of State University of New York Press

Production by Diane Ganeles
Marketing by Fran Keneston

Library of Congress Cataloging-in-Publication Data

Staley, Harry C., 1924–
   Truant pastures : the complete poems of Harry C. Staley / Harry C.
Staley.
      p. cm.
   ISBN 978-1-4384-3834-4 (pbk. : alk. paper)
   I. Title.

PR6069.T189T78 2011
821'.92—dc22   2011003197

10 9 8 7 6 5 4 3 2 1

For Helen

It will remember itself from every sides,
for all gestures,
in each our word

love

— *Finnegans Wake*

Contents

Part II: Therapy (1970–1974)

Part III: Last Years and Nursing Home

Preface

Most of the poems in this book have been collected in *The Lives of a Shell-Shocked Chaplain* and *All One Breath*, but I have included some previously not published.

I have no idea when I began writing poetry. In St. Michael's Diocesan High School my friends and I hung around the journalism room, where I was editor, but quietly wrote poems, a beginning. During my brief semester at St. John's University I once again discovered the room where students produced *Sequoia*, which included poetry as well as short stories and essays. Several of my poems appeared in *Sequoia*. My poetry was influenced by Edward Arlington Robinson and William Butler Yeats. I would return to this activity four years later, years spent in the woods and fields of France, and into Germany. I had volunteered my army membership and was accepted. I was eighteen. By the time I was nineteen, I was engaged in the Battle of the Bulge. After Hitler's fall, we awaited orders to leave for Japan. I created a newspaper and, never seeing a black soldier anywhere near my regiment, wrote an editorial questioning the situation. The editorial created quite a stir and appeared to infuriate my captain. I was to be punished, the punishment was my being sent to Manchester University for the academic year, a blissful period of Shakespeare and James Joyce. I liked the English and they found me the kind of yank they enjoyed knowing. The academic year concluded, I asked to be returned to my "outfit"—Paris. Stutgart, perhaps? Rome? Milan? It was a tour a millionaire's son might have enjoyed. Upon returning, finally, to Brooklyn, I picked up my studies, completing my first degree in two years. My responsibilities to St. John's satisfied, I continued graduate studies at the University of Pennsylvania, where shared courses with Helen Raynes, a dancer with one of

Martha Graham's principal dancers, a writer, and a political activist, whom, in time, I married. My doctoral studies turned to James Joyce in whom I found my years of study of the catechism as useful as did Joyce himself, and led in time, to my PhD, although by then I had been on the faculty of what evolved into the University of the State of New York, where originally I was hired as a one-year replacement for someone on sabbatical which led to the post of Professor of English Literature, a tenure of over forty years, with three separate years at the American College in Paris, an institution that evolved into the American University of Paris. My wife and I spent a year on faculty of Xiamen University in China. However, I continued writing poems.

In 1967 one of my poems received the annual poetry award from the Arizona Quarterly. In 1965 my first book of poems, *The Lives of a Shell-Shocked Chaplain* was published. *All One Breath* was published in 2002. And now *The Complete Poems*, dedicated to Helen Raynes Staley, which I hope you will enjoy.

Introduction I

Judith E. Johnson

In workshops on the creative process, I tell the writers and artists who are learning to reach into their creativity that we bring our entire lives to each moment, and that we can indeed make a book out of the enormous weight of feeling that attaches to our experience. The first workshop I taught on this subject, I had the inestimable good fortune to be team-teaching with Harry Staley, whose talent, creativity, scholarship, and ability to pick up any ball whatsoever and run with it, never ceased to astonish me. Actor, Joyce scholar, nurturing teacher to generations of SUNY at Albany students, the most supportive and enlivening of colleagues, Harry Staley is also one of those extraordinary poets who has brought an entire life to a stunning book published late in his career. In our cultural life at this time and place, we have no easy way to recognize striking talent in artists too modest and sometimes too busy to promote their own work. For years audiences in Albany have had the pleasure of hearing Staley perform these powerful and brilliant poems. The lives of poets do not follow predictable patterns. Sometimes it takes a life to make a book. Sometimes it takes the restraint, the hard apprenticeship, the integrity and determination involved in a rigorous quest for perfection to keep from publishing one's work until it has realized its ideal form. In this book, *The Lives of a Shell-Shocked Chaplain*, Harry Staley has given us the result of such a quest, a life of patient and selfless work for the sake of the art. This publication will enable audiences beyond Staley's immediate surroundings at last to make the acquaintance of a powerful and original poet.

This dazzling narrative and dramatic sequence follows the life of one Charles J. McCaffery from his birth in 1920 to his death in a nursing home in 1987. By the use of this narrative framework, Staley not only enables himself to deal with the rites of passage in the life of an ordinary ethical and decent human being in this nation in this century, but he also enables himself to write a kind of poetic history of the great moments of historical crisis of our time, as seen through the life of an ethical protagonist. Immersed in the historical and cultural detail (films, comedy shows) of our century, McCaffery relives his life as if it had indeed been a film. Service in World War II is the pivotal event in the imaginary McCaffery's life. But through that event, we see refracted the later wars, in particular the war in Vietnam. Because McCaffery is reflecting in his old age upon his entire life, time and history become collapsed, concentrated to one moment of moral choice which is every moment of choice. The compelling vision of these poems is that no event in history happens only in its own time. No decision involves only the elements of that decision. No war is only that war; it carries the common structure and common choices of all wars. And it is this experience, this knowledge that choices that were right in their time may retrospectively and retroactively have been wrong, that drives the protagonist of these poems from shell-shock into that final visionary madness our great cultural myths tell us is also prophetic insanity.

Listen to the fierce rhythms of the opening poem and chant, "Chalk it:" "Chalk it up to chance / to check points to chicken out / to chevrons to chaplains to corpses / chalk the shrewd comedians / chalk Bob Hope and charity." Enjoy the wit, 1920's slang and atmosphere, and formal intricacy of "Noc-turnes (from early films):" "a corpse and several cops/cops and a single corpse / murdered by a christmas gun / complete with gleaming cartridges / for a dollar-forty-nine /at Abraham and Straus . . . / went BLAT, went BLAT-BLAT-BLAT / to register: / one tear in the tux; two holes in the brow; / but never the name of Chuck-the-Avenger, who / always arranged to be known as Pat / when he carried a heater, when he carried a gat."

Encounter McCaffery in his final visionary madness and moral anguish:

"and I believed
whatever weapon pierced my flesh
bullet, shrapnel, sword, or bayonet, renewed
the sacred penetrations that sanctify the world:
      Adam in Paradise
      Cain at the plow
      Mary and her Ghost
      The nails that pinioned Christ
But once in war I came to know
I was outranked by any child
great moonlight bombers slew."

We are proud to be initiating the SUNY and St. Andrews cooperative publishing venture, "Visions and Prophecies" with this compelling poetic debut. It took a lifetime to write *"The Lives of a Shell-Shocked Chaplain."* In it Staley brings his entire life to these prophetic poems.

Chalk It

Chalk it
chalk it all
chalk it all up to the alphabets
to chalk marks to children chewing chocolate
to choosing sides, to cheering Chuck Klein, Charley Root
 to checking the answers

Chalk it
chalk it all
chalk it up to learning what to say
 from Pacelli, Spellman, Sheen, Pius X & XII
  to old men ranting
   to pledge all legions
    to prelates chanting
     in church

Chalk it up to old men checking to find me out
 to well-dressed cops
  to one old man chuckling
   "Greetings to Charles"

Chalk it up to chance
 to check points to chicken out
  to chevrons to chaplains soothing corpses
   chalk the shrewd comedians
    chalk Al Jolson, Bob Hope, and charities

Chalk it up
 to "those great boys: Our boys" and their chums
  face down in the mud
   chilled to the broken bone
    to worms at lunch under choppers churning

to CHARGE FIVE FUSE QUICK SHELL HE
        to chunk to chalk-dust to chunk-chunk to marrow
          to chunk-chunk-chunk to Charlie-six
              to Charley I-read-you I-read-you
                  willco   over   out

And chalk it
      chalk it all
            chalk it up to erasing the board
                and cleaning the erasers
                      to chiding the children
                            and chalking their bones

and chalk it all
      chalk all old men and alphabets
          and chortling cheaters sending greetings
and chalk you
      chalk it all
          chalk you
                chalk it
                      chalk it all

Introduction II

The Pesky Art of Harry C. Staley

George Drew

> In the vestibule Old Father Smith
> who would outlive his troubled sight
> waited for the end of Mass
> to watch the children pass him by,
> his one eye blind, the other sad.

In this stanza we are up against a double whammy: one eye sees nothing, one too much. As such, it easily could be the epigraph to the volume in which it appears, *The Lives of a Shell-Shocked Chaplain*, and to this volume of collected poems. A second volume, also included here, *All One Breath*, continues, in the saga of Thomas Kelly, the protagonist of many of the poems, the paradoxical nature of life and those who live it. In one poem, "Invocation," the speaker exclaims, "Sing, heavenly Moose! Make thou the depth / of swollen midnight darkness visible." There it is, sight confounded by a paradoxical nature. In another poem, "Elegy for Thomas Kelly," the speaker asserts, "We're working to preserve contending versions of your memory." It is precisely this that Harry Staley has done in both his prior two volumes, as well as in the new poems included here, in these collected poems. We need only look closely at his first volume to make the case.

The Lives of a Shell-Shocked Chaplain was published as part of a series called "Visions and Prophecies," which was designed to publish and give recognition to "those prodigious poets whose first books are published late in their careers, carrying in their lines the weight of entire lives lived in the tumult of the actual." Remarkably, success already had been achieved, for though the book was published "late in [his] career," not all the poems were. These are the facts. They are important, but they don't really prepare one for the startling poetic journey that is the work.

In the first line of the first poem of the first section, *Early Times*, Dr. Peters, "Geo-Therapist," says of Charles McCaffery, "As with everyone, his life lies in its recounting." And in this splendid first volume Harry Staley gives us precisely that—a recounting of McCaffery's life, or rather, as the title has it, lives. More to the point, Staley gives us an accounting, period. The poems are lyric in form, some traditional in meter and rhyme, some free verse; strung together, they form a clear narrative that propels us backward and forward in time, dissecting McCaffery's life with haunting language and metaphor. In *Last Years & Nursing Home*, the speaker, whom we can assume is playing Severn to the dying McCaffery's Keats, says of his charge: "The final flight is quite uncertain." What's not uncertain is the trajectory of *The Lives of a Shell-Shocked Chaplain*.

What Dr. Peters calls the "principle of relative reminiscence" is applied full force to McCaffery's "lives." Generally, the trajectory is chronological, from the chaplain's birth in 1920 to his death in 1987. The two sections mentioned, and the second, entitled tellingly *Therapy*, divide the chronology neatly—on the surface. Within this structural linearity occurs the "relative reminiscence" Dr. Peters points to. And in that relativity lies the truth of McCaffery, and of the sweep of the twentieth century. For, besides witnessing his own "lives," McCaffery witnesses all our lives, thus elevating himself into a kind of fractured Tiresias—or perhaps more apt, a male Cassandra to whom no one except his Geo-Therapist will listen. And what, after all, are we to listen to? Like Prufrock, McCaffery "yearns to yearn once more / towards something he has yet to learn, / something brave that he has never done" (from the poem "Immersion"). The way is not clear. But there is a difference: McCaffery is not really Prufrock. He is haunted, but he also is still morally engaged, decent, and a vessel of remembrance, even if jumbled and un-chronological. Memory survives, and thus the hope of redemption, if not outright salvation and grace.

Memory, in *Early Times*, is a smorgasbord of events, real and imagined, Christian iconography, pop culture—especially baseball and film—schools and schoolmasters, and images heroic and otherwise of war—particularly World War II, the true defining experience of McCaffery's life, and one of several wars (Korea, Vietnam, Latin America) that provide the nightmare web of events and hallucinatory imagery that haunts McCaffery's imagination. As McCaffery himself says in "Early Gothic," "His eye is on the spasm." Literally, he means orgasm; symbolically, he means much more than sex. As he says in "About the Aeneid," he "contemplate[s] the grammar, not the pain, / of burning bones and vengeance." In the second section, *Therapy*, the intertwining of motifs established in *Early Times* continues, deepening into a poetic harrowing of a haunted man, and validating Dr. Peter's assertion that McCaffery was one priest who "should not have been sent either to Korea, or Latin America, or Vietnam." To say the least, this is classic understatement. And yet it misses the point, too. McCaffery's life, in the end, is both informed and redeemed by such awful experience. And he knows it.

So do we, once we read the third section, *Last Years & Nursing Home*. In "The Unknown General: Souvenirs (1978)," McCaffery says it most poignantly:

> But once in war I came to know
> I was outranked by any child
> great moonlight bombers slew.

Compare this knowledge, this consciousness (which can occur only at the expense of an utter extinguishment of the Self and its self-importance), with that revealed in the first section of a poem called "Nocturnes" from *Early Times*. The section is titled "Dog-Fight." McCaffery is eight years old, and he is lying on his bed imagining himself as some kind of Red Baron who is dispatching various enemy aircraft while "God, the Grown-Up, watches from afar." This is war romanticized by a child, but it's what occurs in the last five lines that is so terrifyingly significant:

At P.S. 4

I swoop and fire on the teaching staff,
wound the principal, bank and swerve
east-north-east to battered Armentiere
where, spying frightened relatives I strafe
and watch them flee across the bedroom floor.

Like hallucinogenic colors melting one into the other, here enemy, God, teachers, principal, and relatives blend into an apocalypse of eradication. It's a brilliant moment in a brilliant poem about childhood and its demons, which ultimately metamorphose into very real adult demons—the kind that terrorized a good chunk of the twentieth century. But it's precisely this actualization of childhood fantasy that allows for the development of the agonized adult we encounter in the first excerpt. Between these two totemic poems is the story of Charles McCaffery's "lives" strung.

In his blurb on the back cover of *The Lives of a Shell-Shocked Chaplain*, novelist William Kennedy quotes the following lines: "maggots cleanse the battlefield, / leaving bits of boneshine." These come from the poem "Dark Cubes" and are synoptic of what this book, *All One Breath*, and the new poems in this volume, are trying to bear witness to. Finally, *The Lives of a Shell-Shocked Chaplain* is that rarest of books, one that, through the power of language poetically charged, moves the protagonist and us—the readers, the eavesdroppers—toward a transcendence, or rather, its possibility. McCaffery, in "Nursing Home," is on his deathbed. A recurrent figure throughout the book, Sister Thomasine, sits beside him in section 6, "McCaffery's Bardo," "chaste and in her twenties once again." But it is the unnamed speaker (Dr. Peters?) who witnesses the chaplain's "final flight" from "penultimate Miami." As the section ends, the speaker fixes our attention on the possibility of transcendence, telling us that while Sister Thomasine calls to the chaplain "shrilly by his family name,"

> . . . he flew far beyond her angry voice
> to find behind the bounds of Paradise
> the truant pastures of eternity,
> nameless as Miami to a bird.

McCaffery's Paradise, like the final flight itself, is uncertain. But there is nothing uncertain about the art of Harry Staley. Technically, his work is masterful. Yet technique, no matter how superb, is not enough. Ultimately, it is vision and commitment to it that separates pretenders from legitimate heirs. If this volume of collected poems is daunting in its iconography, its historicity, and its Joycean wordplay, its rewards for the persistent reader are clear: a deep compassion heightened into grace through the powerful medium of a pesky art called poetry.

The Lives of a Shell-Shocked Chaplain: Charles McCaffery (b. 1920, d. 1978)

*the record is fragmentary,
the soft tissues are gone, leaving mainly bones*
—Gerald M. Edelman

Part I
Early Times

Preliminary Report from Dr. Peters, Geo-therapist

As with everyone, his life lies in its recounting. He is in our nursing-home, now, composing his life.

What matters is the afterthought, the creative, mendacious afterthought. Auto-psychographal concoctions. He rides through every weather, bikes through blizzards, swims through hurricanes, bats fungoes in the fog. Occasionally, like Julius Caesar, he recounts his exploits in the Third Person Singular.

It is worth noting, incidently, that he dates the events of his life quite tendentiously. It is worth noting, as well, that his most telling insights occur within a twilight of mind, a mental crepuscule, hypnogogic, on either quivering edge of sleep. He thinks of them as nocturnes. I would say he's better at bed than bed-rock.

Penmanship (1931, 1984)

OOOOOOOOOOOOOOOOOOOOOOOOOOOOOO
IIIIIIIIIIIIIIIIIIIIIIIIIIIIIIIIIIIIIIIIIIIIIIIIIIIIIIII

He (I) dipped the pen-nib into the blue ink-well,
inscribing all we'd need to know
in lovely cursive servile script.

He (I) trained in Palmer-Method
ovals and pushpulls
by the Sisters of the Iron Cross

aware of sin slithering near
beautifully tattooed
(ovals and pushpulls).

Nuns and pupils (we) drove the serpent off
with quick ejaculations, and God (numinous, austere)
forgave.

Already longing backward from my future, he (I)
wooed my approbation, mine and all the tall appraisers,
nuns and priests and God (ubiquitous), everywhere,

everywhere, their evaluating stare:

in sleep,
with Vera, Mary, Grace and Gloria, tracing ovals;
he (I) making pushpulls

in dreams,
he (I) hid in oval shell-holes;
then, brave in no-man's-land, he (I) push

metal bayonets into German guts, and pull
the wet blade free
before we wake and wash
and walk to school.

Argument from Design (1933, 1980, 1930)

In the damp sockets of Charles' eyes moves an image,
plump maggots scavenging a turtle shell
forty-seven years ago, a bright ceramic
cleansed by scavengers.

Succulent in its cranium his brain survives,
at times considering
commonplace concavities:

sweaty thimbles, salad bowls and pots,
gutted cantaloupes "with worry rinds
and reddish orange flesh," nutshells,
umbrellas, Yankee Stadium;

suddenly again, from nearly fifty years ago,
the front-page picture of a fallen "Chinaman,"
mouth wide open,
his skull as yet within his skin
beside an empty helmet.

Nocturnes (from early films)

1. Dog-Fight (1928)

Through the quiet bedroom's ruthless skies
I fly my Fokker . . . Camel on my tail
detonated by an Albatros . . .
I dispatch three spads . . . blimps burst and all
night long Teutonic conflagrations scar
the dark around the cockpit in my cot,
while God, the Grown-up, watches from afar
the fall of sparrows, Cambrai, Camelot,
and the Cites of the Plain. At P.S. 4
I swoop and fire on the teaching staff,
wound the principal, bank and swerve
east-north-east to battered Armentiere
where, spying frightened relatives, I strafe
and watch them flee across the bedroom floor.

2. Autopsy (1928)

a corpse and several cops
cops and a single corpse
murdered by a christmas gun
complete with gleaming cartridges
for a dollar-forty-nine
at Abraham & Straus . . .
went BLAT, went BLAT-BLAT-BLAT
into four little wells of brimming blood
and the courage of the victim trickled out
complicating quietly the colors of the rug
turning dark and dry before the cops arrived.

to copy down:
one tear in the tux; two holes in the brow;

but never the name of Chuck-the-Avenger, who
always arranged to be known as Pat
when he carried a heater, when he carried a gat.

3. Double Feature (1929)

All afternoon Charles chewed and swallowed,
savoring carnage, the glitter of wounds,
malignant hoofs and heels,
the cry of Redskins feared by starlets
pale as the Virgin Mary

***   ***   ***

After the hun plunged burning back to earth
dark syrup, a sinister trickle,
seeped from the pilot's lip
thickened slowly down his chin
like coagulated chocolate
licked in early evening
all the way home.

4. All Quiet on the Western Front (1932)

Unspent bullets, bright as gems, mean
as teeth, threaten the silence, season
the darkness, potent sculpture, biding
in the bedroom

the alarm-clock holds

snipers fire from windowsills,
cannon from the mantleshelf,
bullets zip past glittering spiked helmets,
long Zeppelins ignite, towers tremble, totter, fall.

a long explosion   furtive silence   shame

a final discharge   armistice and shame

soft, spent silence,

shame

Services (1929)

I.

After Black Thursday the light began to change.
October grew dim in offices and stores
and the nervous eyes of relatives.

Sunday Charles attended Children's Mass,
lulled by Latin; carefully Young Father Smith
revealed the host,
omnipotent and bright,
larger than a quarter.

In the vestibule Old Father Smith
who would outlive his troubled sight
waited for the end of Mass
to watch the children pass him by,
the one eye blind, the other sad.

II. Vietnam, 1966

Even as I hold aloft the unscarred disk
I understand the holy rage of Cain
who laid the harvest of his heart,
the yield of earth and seed,
bloodless wine and bloodless grain,
before the sanguinary eye of God

who found such sacrifice unworthy of his name
and vouchsafed his regard
on Abel's immolated Lamb,
a slaughtered creature, its shy heart stilled
to satisfy the hungers of the Lord.

The transubstantiated host holds Christ de-stigmatized:
the wounds are gone,
the wine won't scab, the bread won't scar,
there's nothing there for Thomas' hand to touch
unlike the bodies of the faithful, kneeling here
and swallowing; whose warm and mortal blood
absorbs the sacrament, and courses on a little longer.

Biology One (1934, 1957)

Brother Gilbert intoned: "Boys, Ah boys!
Remember Ruth, and forget about old Darwin."

who was, we knew, an atheist and kinda foreign
and claimed we came from apes
who came from fish who learned to fly
or crawl and climb old trees and then climb down again
and learned to walk upright and use the thumb
and think and talk and master Latin
and pitch and HIT HOME RUNS, "Ah, the Babe, boys!"

Just last night, still hearing him, I sank through sleep
and illiterate leagues of ancient oceans, down
to the salty womb of everyone. There
a killer whale, deeply aloft, aware of spotlights
shining in high night,
stares through tides and surging centuries,
metamorphoses and nests, spires and temporary towers,
soaring chambers of power deeply aloft in high night
above the last vast evaporation and the blank
obituaries of

tigers orioles cardinals cubs
giants indians senators reds
braves pirates
Boston, Brooklyn, Washington, New York:
THE YANKEES, "Ah, the Babe!"

Take Us In, Mister? (1930's, 1944)

(Chanted by children in front of movie houses, imploring passersby of legal age to take their money and buy the tickets for them)

One hot day an old man with bad teeth, a tough tattoo
and a scary smile, gave us our tickets
one to me, one to Jack McKay,
winked twice and walked away.

Inside, Buster Crabbe, young, decent, dead,
and tied to the saddle of a terrified horse,
galloped home across the plains.

TAKE US IN, MISTER?

far from the jungle where Buster Crabbe
swung through the trees, protecting natives
and killing malevolent beasts.

TAKE US IN, MISTER?

far from Mars and luminous castles
where Buster scorned the allure
of Princess Aura.

TAKE US IN, MISTER?

Buster Crabbe survived like Jesus Christ,
to be observed in separate apparitions.

TAKE US IN, MISTER?

far from the tropical sniper in a literal tree
who sighted Corporal John McKay
serial number 1 2 1 5....3....7....3....

Asymptote (1945)

(A line which continually approaches a given curve, but
does not meet it within a finite distance.)

You must remember this as time goes by:

as time goes by there'll come a time
when time will start to STOP going by
and when it stops the bogeys go
but that won't matter,
you won't know.

*** *** ***

In April 1944
Cpl. Cyril Marowitz tore
the limbs and head from a musical doll
(dressed in a German uniform)

He spared its trunk so we all could hear
the pain of its delicate tune.
Marowitz died of artillery vibes
on a noisy afternoon,
nobody noticed the doll was gone.

*** *** ***

It's still the same old story:

You can't know the locus of a point, kid,
where the crazy curve of life, kid,
hits the crazy line of death.

*** *** ***

Bogey an imaginary source of fear
Bogey a bugbear
Bogey an evil goblin
Bogey a screen image that is unidentified, but hostile

Le Bourget (1946)

Shopping in the A&P,
McCaffery comes upon Charles Augustus Lindbergh,
slim, bitter, transparent,
between McCaffery and the frozen foods.

As a child,
McCaffery knew the dead sometimes return,
agonized transparencies,
part fog, part mist, and cold,
their neglected anguish unresolved,
despairing through the space of living people's
living dreams.

But now while politicians plan
to renovate the rubbled towns and decorate
or camouflage vacated concentration camps,
McCaffery knows the dead do not return,
and when he wakes from post-war sleep,

ignores the implications of his dreams.
At the laundromat
he watches swirling windows,
while Lindbergh,
once more in mid-flight,
with every searchlight in the target field
yearning west, hears spectral voices
come to guide him through the dark
toward Europe where the votaries of Thule
publicize the Protocols of Zion.

Unlike ghosts
heroes in their lost and legendary space
perform forever, abetting certain patriotic minds.

Even now, this solid morning in Atlantic Avenue,
McCaffery stands outside YE TOY & HOBBY SHOP,
gazing at a fragile monoplane,
his face transparent on the storefront glass.

Engagement (1949, 1917)

In shallow sleep
Charles hears again the old explosive skies of childhood:
jam-tin in hand, he races from a wall of fire, falls
somewhere near the Somme stranded on barbed wire,
all night long hallucinating peace,
quiet homes restored to timeless girls,
every wound and wall and window healed
and lovely women offer yet again
soft white feathers to sensitive young men
who hear the drone of future bombing planes
(all bass and baritone, fatherly, avuncular)
Freidrichsafen
      Handley-Page
            Gotha
                 Stuka
                     Lancaster
                         B-29

in valiant moonlight raids
murdering a girl who hated
ovaltine
her total memory spilling out in viscid lumps
intimate images drying off
as lofty brave vibrations soften toward the west,
beyond a billboard standing tall, and smoking:

LUCKY STRIKE GREEN HAS GONE TO WAR

Near Bellau Woods, Verdun, and Anzio
the words of Sister Thomasine
explain subtraction:
minuend subtrahend difference or remainder
minuend subtrahend difference or remainder
minuend subtrahend difference or remainder

Aging in the local Legion Hall
near Charles McCaffery's dream
veterans of old battlefields recall
skinny copulations, scored on week-end pass
long ago in lovely Fayetteville.

Part II

Therapy
(1970–1974)

"Peace on earth!" was said. We sing it.
And pay 2 million priests to bring it.
After two thousand years of mass
We've got as far as poison gas.
—Thomas Hardy

When I was a child my friends and I would play in the clean dry ratless trenches of World War I, where the wounded shed playblood, and after we shot enough bullets and threw enough grenades and fired enough cannons, the living and the dead got up and walked home to their parents.

—Fr. Charles McCaffery, Christmas Sermon 1971

Immersion

He still dreams he's learning how to swim
while grown-ups on the beach
encourage him.

These days he dreams alone; no one on the shore,
breathing ordinary air,
needs or cares to care.

He yearns to yearn once more
towards something he has yet to learn,
something brave that he has never done,
rehearsed in dreams and then
performed at last by day.

He tends to sleep through shallow waters now
far from the deepest volumes where
deep-sea scrawls
hold tales of tide-lost gallantries
read by children,

not by him. He sounds the depths in vain
and, nothing fathomed, surfaces to dawn.

Casualties

When Buster Crabbe died inside my sound track
I hid beside a rigid and eroding cow
far beneath a sleek metallic shark shrieking through
ecstasies of counter-battery,
diving toward MY SKULL.

an abrupt blazing impact, centrifugal & in-
different rage of power, eradicating cartilage & marrow
& gelatinous convolutions,
burst & oblivion simultaneous, nothing
left to stiffen or decay,
my sensuous center senselessly dispersed
until the ruthless parousia counter-clocks the world
restoring all the bits of bone & skin & flesh & fat
& stone-cold bovine carcasses & senile Buster Crabbe,

exposing every idle word or deed, or lust or thought
that tainted my once-demolished brain

& confronting me with every broken boy
I blessed for battle.

Sacrifications

(bless/bles/ . . . fr. O.E. bletsion fr. blod, blood; fr. the use of blood in consecration)

out of cave, slit-trench, grave, they come
into my sleeping brain, caked blood bathed in surplus
very flairs,
    respectful uncertain unanointed

      ***

           their guts once
           stank like glistening garbage

           I bless them
           a lover here, a lover there,
           lifts a voice in prayer,
           asking God to spare
           this one, just this one, spare
           this one . . .

           I bless them all

    ***

[Geo. Peters offers the following information
from Mayan history:
Bloodletting and sacrification played a leading part in religious
observance. Blood was drawn from the nose, the forehead,
the cheeks, the lower lips, the elbows, arms, thighs and legs,
and the private parts. The blood thus obtained, as well as that
of sacrificial victims, human as well as animal, was liberally
sprinkled over their idols.]

    ***

. . . live-stock, trench meat, drying
inside my brain. Hadn't they sensed
the burly sergeants folding flags
                    after Taps
                        after harmless blank
                            salvos?

                    I bless them.

      ***

                    . . . a lover here, a lover there,
                    lifts a voice in prayer
                    begging God to spare
                    this one, just this one, spare
                    this one.

      ***

[Peters, again:
The perforations and cutting instruments used in these blood-
letting rites were . . . knives and blades made of flint, obsid-
ian, bones, and shell.]

                    I bless them all!

Dark Cubes

But of the cities of these people,
which the Lord thy God doth give thee
for an inheritance, thou shalt
save alive nothing that breatheth:
But thou shalt utterly destroy them

        —Deut. 20:16

In one dark cube or another, in the movies, in the bedroom,
my old dreams batter humanity,
an almost anonymous slaughter with a few elegant names,
Ayres, Baxter, Bosworth, Clive . . .

 Dr. Oscar Homolka, the psychoanalist,
 warned of rage in heaven and homicidal paranoia,
 but nobody guessed his sweating hysteria
 possessed a Balkan truth even as silver Zeppelins
 eased, smooth, through cold space,
 nudging darkness, piercing night,
 toward Paris, London, toward our diocese,
 into dreams between the walls, between the wars.
 Spaniards slaughter Spaniards in fiction, film, and barrio,
 while *THE HINDENBURG* sails east.
 And later, somewhere else (between the walls),
 paratroops descend like doomsday angels
 killing sinners, sparing saints:
 choirs of maggots cleanse the battlefield
 leaving bits of boneshine
 unlike splattered shreds of flesh and muddy corpses
 left to dry in Belleau Woods
      and nothing like the living frog
 I killed in Summer 1932, a lump
 of soggy camouflage, her astounded eyes the size
 of BB's that, *phump-phump*, did the job
 in the lovely light of early afternoon.

Morning Song

. . . then *pit* inside my sleep, slight,
isolated, *pit*, then another outside,
sharp, isolated, like battle opening beyond the windowpane,
light rain, hesitant, uncertain,
drops deepen like open vowels,
farther back and lower in the throat,
pit, bled, blood,
they concentrate, rattling under
high rounds of thunder
blasting overhead
like battles fought from soft seats
in the movies of my childhood,
artillery mixed with musketry
killing scores of valiant youth
in blazing black-and-white

      in nineteen forty-four "somewhere in France,"
      Norton Ipswich Alexander,
      whom we privates and corporals called
      Ipswich
      because we liked the sound of it,

           died

      his real, three-dimensional jaw torn away, the blood
      spread red, searching cold space
      for something warm to heal
      flesh, or cartilage, or bone, somewhere in France,

      his death, I remember,
      was the very first of very few
      in a quiet sector

movie wounds are frightful, but
I don't know what Norton felt, fading quick, unlike
the film star, draped on barbed wire all night long,
while other actors pray for him to die

dignified generals praise their dead; sometimes
I try to picture them with shattered jaws, like Norton,
or this morning's mouse, taut and cooling in the trap.

That might be what woke me just before the storm,
something in another room
went like *that*

Apochrypha

Genesis
far from sunlight dark fish suck and gulp
sometimes almost waking I remember

Resurrection
the wounds dried in the tomb
bearded and battered the son emerged
ready to rally the fugitives

John
in the be- buh- . . . in
the beginning was the . . . what . . .
was the wuh- the wuh- . . . in the
bub- . . . bub- . . . in the be-
. . . ginning was the . . . what? . . . the what?
in the . . .

About the Aneid

Exoriare aliquis nostris ex ossibus ultor
(Arise some avenger from our bones.)

Although my mastery of Latin fades,
that Queen translates herself forever
into fire, an angry light
for cold imperiled voyagers;
that classic blaze dims down
to prosody and syntax
fluttering in dactyls.

And I, a later voyager, over fifty years adrift,
contemplate the grammar, not the pain,
of burning bones and vengeance;
I who claim to be incensed
about the burning bones in MyLai,
after Belsen, Nagasaki, Watts,
and Washington.

What then of Dido's pyre? She
and the language of her love are dead
while the modern fires seethe
where proud and pious syllables
(El Salvador, Granada, Concepcion, Colon)
mark the reach of recent empire.

Aliquis . . . ultor? Some avenger?

From the holy ash of "pagan" bones, napalmed far away,
let some surviving love
redeem the years of sacrilege
while we God-fearing Christians study all night long
to parse the meaning of our bombs.

Mother Behold Thy Son

I

. . . almost napping, i enjoyed the feel
of rubber–sheeting underneath. i saw
the shiny cloth around christ's loins
in the crucifix beyond my mother's chair. Her eyes
above black headlines
were watching me.
I closed my
LET YOUR DICKEY ALONE
own eyes
TAKE YOUR HAND AWAY
it wasn't
FROM THERE
there
TAKE IT AWAY
but i couldn't
LET GO
let go unless
DID YOU HEAR
i grabbed it to show
WHAT I SAID
she wasn't wrong
DID YOU HEAR
and held it to show she wasn't wrong
WHAT I SAID
while she came toward me

II

Vagabonds
It might have been late dusk, maybe 1934,
big letters, Argon? Neon? Red? Ivory? Blue?

began to glow against a sudden autumn snow,
that fell, for all I knew,
upon the homeless of the year.

I think I see a "bum" beside the movie house,
eyes shut tight against the cold, one hand out
in supplication, the other clutched
against his crotch.

Soft flakes, each indifferent and "unique,"
seem to float through layers of ocean.
I can hardly read the cold Marquee:

PRIVATE WORLDS . . . ?
A THOUSAND LEAGUES BENEATH THE SEA . . . ?

Early Gothic

Remember adolescence?
mired in masturbation,   secret years
of solipsistic orgies. Think:
His eye is on the spasm.

Sr. Thomasine rebuked our tearless eyes as she,
wallowing in pain and piety, her angry lenses
flashing grief,

described
the grisly bloody tortured death of Christ one thunderous
Friday afternoon years and years and years ago
and RIGHT NOW this rainy Wednesday morning
GOD
once colorless odorless tasteless lighter than air
hangs NOW
only thirty years or so
after Christmas and the cold night of Epiphany
after scores of paupers and poppas played Santa

GOD
made up as Christ, bruised and torn and stretched
(ambiguously moribund),

and we murder Him with sin
gazing at Grace Black, Mary Fleisch, Vera Potter, Gloria
Gales
(in their precocious loveliness),
We, prolong and share the very act of sacrilege,
of deicide and desire
done by Adam, done by Eve,
who brought original filth into the stainless world
we, Adam-and-Eve; we, Grace, Mary, Vera, Gloria; and we
who gaze at them,
longing.

Tidings (Christmas 1930s, 1973)

Having missed the early plane to Endicott,
I heard the engines hum and roar
and watched what looked like oil-slicks in my cup.
I missed the safe geography I'd learned in school
and hymns my classmates sang in unison.

I missed the cheap electric train that turned
and turned and turned

(from ENDicott to WAVerly & BINGhamton
      & ITHaca
& BINGhamton & WAVerly and HOME again
to ENDicott beneath the Christmas Tree),

transporting nervous relatives in shabby overcoats
and sweaty hats, who drank from cardboard coffee-cups.
The kind of men who
missed

sleek model planes that roamed out loud
through epic corridors at home, when I,
the GOGGLE ACE, held bombers in my hand,
my humming heard in Flanders Fields and Hollywood,
humming over table-tops and chairs,
over Dresden, London, Nagasaki, Troy,
humming after trains near Endicott.

Contractions

As I grew tall God shrank
like Uncle Bill who worked for Tel & Tel

word spread through wires,
where sometimes birds perched and sang,
until his world turned deaf and dis-
connected

but not before his sister Lil,
young and coughing in her convent room
where she was known as Sister Mary Charles
died in a white winter after World War I,
called a long-distance beyond the moon,
past Mars, past Jupiter, past every pagan planet,
through "wireless ether" to her Fatherly God
who long ago uttered the first hello.
She died, absolved and sanctified,
bequeathing me her pious name.

Word moves underground through buried wires now,
and I, who once believed in Genesis, believe
silent galaxies expand inside
the smallest, smoothest tide-washed stone.

Ex-Capt. McCaffery

[neon n. symbol Ne A rare, inert, gaseous element occurring in the atmosphere to the extent of 18 parts per million and obtained by fractured distillation of liquid air. It is colorless but glows reddish-orange in an electrical discharge. From Greek, neuter of neos: *new.]*

In the Depression my Father marched
six days a week through city streets
selling neon signs that burned
like spots of fever in the night.

Veteran of THE WAR,
(Captain of the Post Exchange, Camp Meade, Baltimore)
now out of uniform and hoping for
another war:
officer privileges, officer's pay.

When Hitler's troops went storming through the Corridor,
Father yearned;
when Tojo triumphed in Corregidor,
Father yearned.

But by then
Father, nearly fifty-four,
had grown too old to serve again.

He inflated. Reconciled to peace.
Barely wrinkled, totally unscarred,
he drifted toward a private no-man's-land,
his memory seeping out from year to year;
and that's how I remembered him: nothing burst,
his world soughed peacefully away.

Last night I saw him, bouyancy restored, lighter than air,
ascending gently through the atmosphere,
above the latest neon dimmed by dawn,
higher now than history, far beyond
Auschwitz, or Palermo, or Verdun,
above the Spad or Messerschmitt or Zeppelin,
rising undiminished and at large
through silent daylight toward the roaring sun.

Fr. Charles Visits Athens

My soul shall be satisfied as with marrow and
fatness: and my mouth shall praise thee . . .
                                          —Psalms 63:5

With all his bones well-fleshed, the flesh well-clothed,
he came to the Acropolis.
Across the cracks he walked, happy in his fat;
there was damp marrow in his bones; neither gland
nor cell nor artery nor anything inside
lay dry to toxic light like plinth or pillar.

He sauntered smug among the ruins until
the filling from a tooth dislodged itself.

He spat it on the older fragments, spent the night
dreaming of a throbbing Parthenon
X-rayed on a screen and analyzed
by Seward D. MacDougal, D.D.S.

Seward spoke of root and crown, enamel, gum,
of old decay and calcium,
of caries and caryatids.
Seward quoted from the O.E.D.:
       Mental . . . 1. Pertaining to the jaw
       Mental . . . 2. Pertaining to the mind
Seward talked of faults in every kind of ossature
and warned of mal-
       occlusion . . . the action of occluding or . . .
       of stopping up, of closing . . .

Offertory

facing away from the people behind me I started to doubt
and the people looking at my chasuble "the color of budding
and living vegetation" whispered in ordinary language

O Lord I am not worthy

facing them I held the thin small white concoction some of
them shut their eyes in abnegation and some squinted and
some stared at the sphere of the lord pleading for indulgence
swift unshed and untransubstantiated blood pulsing through their
veins and I interpreted for them in proud latin *domine non sum
dignis* staring at the cardboard christ

I the holy veteran commenced to doubt seeing again profane blood
and rolling viscera steaming in daylight "far and forgot" and the
soaken torn camouflage

and garbed in linen silk damask embroidery I faced the altar
and completed the cleanly sacrifice
nothing slaughtered gutted skewered no stigma no sacramental
scars no nail marks no pierced thorax no rosary or thorns around
the head I celebrated the sacrifice before this sunday flock who had
never seen me bless a young man, blood seeping through
olive drab

Caw

I try to hold my sleep against the dawn

I sleep against the outside light where crows
(nuns and Sergeants   priests and colonels)
conspire in the brightening yard
calling me from play   calling me from flight
back through the pillow   calling me from flight
beyond Saigon, beyond Hanoi, and Seoul
calling me from flight
I fly high beyond the call
cursing God for every shattered wall

I sleep against the clarifying day   against a plebiscite
of murdered selves   forgotten relatives and mean
authorities bleeding friends parents and parishioners
conspiring with a squad of crows
to call me back again   to call me down
to call me back to call and   call and call

Paradoxology

I

On the metal box of chocolate walks a boy
holding a metal box of chocolate where the boy
walks and holds again the metal box:
side upon side upon side, he never stops,
grows that way small and this way large.

I've become illiterate of space. Sophistries
of magnitude confuse, ambiguous
as dream. What works the utter volume of the world
whirls and widens heedlessly away.

Even so, the boy and box hold still,
infinite and two-dimensional.

Words contrive the violent range of galaxies
this way small and that way large
raging in spans of farther galaxies
answering the time
when words first shaped the sacred orbs of space,
shaped God, our Shaper, once.

II

About the metal box:
That tin wall with all its pseudo-vanishing
like dreams in dreams of dreamers dreaming

It's all about chocolate

I remember a balloon rising, rising,
that way small, concentrating altogether out
into other, farther blue

boy gone, dream gone, balloon blown
out

all matter, ourself or anything,
shrunk to senseless energy

emptied events
like yesterdays reducing in the memory, that way small
and almost colorless, or soon
darker than chocolate

I'm the infinite boy I left and the last
frustration of mothering zero
comes this way large.

Voltages and a Fading Coal

> . . . *a spiritual state very like to*
> *that cardiac condition which the Italian*
> *physiologist Luige Galvani, using a*
> *phrase almost as beautiful as Shelley's,*
> *called the enchantment of the heart*
> —Stephen Dedalus

Once in June
lightning rang my telephone

Once in childhood
I touched a socket with my fingertips
and felt omnipotence
buzzing through my bone

Late in the Enlightenment
damp muscles in Galvani's frog
twitched and shuddered to the charge
of a "weak metallic arc"

In the eighteen-hundreds Emerson spoke of *dream-power*
transcending all limit and privacy
by virtue of which
a man is a conductor of
the whole river of electricity

In the Summer of 1953 the radio announced
Ethel and Julius Rosenberg had been
electrocuted

post-mortem examinations of electrocuted criminals
revealed
a number of interesting phenomena

the temperature of the body rose promptly after death
the heart
at first flaccid when exposed
gradually contracted and assumed a tetanized condition

the blood was profoundly altered biochemically
it was of a very dark color
and rarely coagulated

Sometimes at night
something in my head goes PING
a brainspark blows my dream;
I wake to smokeless dark
unscorched
and turn to find my love

Part III

Last Years
and
Nursing Home

Final Diagnosis

[coded for colleagues by Dr. Peters, Resident Geo-therapist]

The layers broke up into smaller and smaller pieces.
Earthquakes fractured them.

In time the rock's internal stresses
popped off a chunk here and there
with help from

ice
prying cracks open and

acid
softening the seams.

When the pieces were small enough
the wind or rain moved them away.

All the pieces get small enough.
It's just a matter of time.

Fish, Two Grown-Ups, Christ (1975)

I shave this semblance of my Father's face
and staunch some blood my razor caught

I see him on his knees one brilliant summer afternoon
building us a dock with nails and wood
where later on I caught and scraped and gutted fish.

That sacrifice of living time and flesh,
the nails and wood, and now my bit of blood,
revive the rage of Sister Thomasine,
rigorous nun, whose reading of the death of Christ
set her eyes aflame with blame.

Father and nun. Digested by the earth long since,
they sift through particles
of sand, perhaps, or wood, or the knees of penitents,
or even through the drifting heft of fish
like those I imaged in the hearth last night,
orange perch, shadowy bass, minnows smoldering,
and near the bottom, wall-eyes glittering.

Sister Thomasine, I no longer cry for Christ;
I see my father in my aging face,
I staunch our blood.

The Unknown General: Souvenirs (1978)

His face is staring there among the bric-a-brac,
clearly General Staff
surviving in a two-inch photograph
framed in flaming red, a souvenir
slightly marred by soft white stains
like floating smoke above old battlefields.
He's donned his medals,
an imperial row, now indistinct and dim,
but neatly pinned.

      In childhood
and through most of puberty, I dreamed
I would be brave in the fine smoke of battle,
and loved by healthy girls whose flesh I'd spare
by wounding other flesh

      and I believed
whatever weapon pierced my flesh,
bullet, shrapnel, sword, or bayonet, renewed
the sacred penetrations that sanctify the world:

      Adam in Paradise
      Cain at the plow
      Mary and her Ghost
      The nails that pinioned Christ

But once in war I came to know
I was outranked by any child
great moonlight bombers slew

I stare against the calm unsparing stare
of this old general and hear historic sounds
of bomb and shell applauding through his brain.

Viaticum (1979)

Just then things brightened in the rain, as though
mere earth in face and flower shown from a private glow
that made the sun irrelevant. At forty-two

I watched a young man gather in
his final light through dull eyes down
to shocked recesses; and I know he must have seen,
as I anointed him,
            the frightend spector of my face.

Not obsessed with death, I sometimes go
through lovely light, certain of the sun.
Fearless and preoccupied I gaze

serenely out, forgetting how I owe
a mortal gesture, pious or obscene,
back across the many-colored days.

Person-To-Person (1979)

The phone rang, hysterical syllables, nonsense.
"JANE . . . verdure drying toward the fall"?
then another said ". . . departed peacefully:
numb in a coma." Peaceful? *in nomine* . . . parted?
and then, lucid,
"McCaughlin's parlor . . . St. Ephrem's . . . You'll
say the . . . ? Saturday . . ." Dead
syllables murmured over marble, *Domine, non sum dignis*
I thought of "verdure" drying toward
the fall
in late summer childhood familiar grass
merely green when we were worthy
we were worthy
we were

    ***

Jane,
the compensating words they made us memorize
so many years ago are almost lost, almost
inaudible *"mea culpa, mea culpa,* most grievous
fault . . ."

but I recall a certain silence
shared in winter once:
waves frozen, suspended in their summer shape,
glowing crest and trough, transfixed.

Wondering, we stared, together and delighted
in that cold.

Whenever I feel young enough to want to learn
I try to see it there in front of us
wordless and aglow.

Abortions (1979)

He has bent his bow like an enemy: He . . . slew all
that were pleasant to the eye in the tabernacle of the
daughter of Zion.

—Lamentations 2:4

That was how she died and would I "celebrate
the mass . . ."
and find the words to purge?
find atoning images to help us understand
the spector or a dark and bloodied room?

or understand the ravaging of God since the first
fierce and holy horn purged redundant
screams of slaughter
in the "cities of the nations
the Lord your God is giving you"?

or understand the shadow of the cross beneath a bomber
trembling against the savaged earth
toward pagans hiding with their children?

I might begin,
"Long before the testament of Zion,
the ocean, deaf and innocent,
began the risk of wombing. Life seeds on
despite whatever flesh is torn
in bed or battlefield. Despite . . ."
From a corner of my room two birds,
healthy in their cage, begin to sing,
dry swells of sound,
neither clarion, nor serenade, nor requiem.

Parakeet and Pilot (1979)

Nearly dead, she will not sing her flight, this trifle
in the corner of the room,
losing the little heat that all the living lose.

Unlike my childhood dream of flight,
decades ago: the helpless *ALBATROS*, gaudy fuselage aflame,
propeller feathering,
burning back to earth in Europe's smoke
while I salute and roar away.

Now, a cold bird gone,
I clean the cage.

Halloween

It's late enough, my private ghosts and guisers have withdrawn,
they beg no more, play no more pranks;
the past has stopped arriving,
even in my dreams. A spectral absence haunts
me now, near dawn.

Saints succeed in their indifferent way.
They've nothing to resolve in these old haunts;
they've left the neighborhood
for good.
   What creaks and shimmers through the walls
is hardly holy, hardly sinister,
a beam, perhaps, or stair, or banister,
innocent, aging, crepitant.

Meantime the pumpkin grins upon the windowsill,
seedless, plump, and like the rest of us
(save ghosts and saints, or souls
burning in purge or doom), like the rest of us,
bio-degradable.
   Above his toothless grin, eyes
glitter, giddy, through the glass.

*** *** ***

Just before I slept, I thought I heard,
oh, somewhere past the edge of town,
a red stag roar in late October rut.

Late Winters

1. This Cold

This cold, he knew, was only seasonal.
All things held still and centering,
wood tightened in the trees and wall,
earth hardened in the hollow and the hill:
mere wintering.

In that moment of the mute and beautiful
he heard across the cold a shallow call,
that held the heat and need of some lone animal,
drift soft and wandering.

2. That Year's Moon

That year's moon went wild with autumn, caught
some men alone and made them mad.
He was alone, but he was winter-wise
and kept indoors to nourish what he had
of warmer memory against the last surprise
that had to come to make his memory naught.

He had a hearth and bed and one large chair,
and all his friends lacked shadows, sat austere,
awaiting amends he'd set his mind to make
as priest, as friend, and from a recent fear
that they were more than shadowless. The lake
began to thaw, snow smoked; he held them there.

Then winter was, like him, another thing
old. And with the warmth he let them go,
unsatisfied with his apologies.
The empty chair, dark hearth, and vernal flow
sent him to bed without his memories.
The icicles cracked and died with spring.

In the Nursing-Home

1. The Senile General in the Garden

hears the names of flowers bursting out
from war-games in his childhood "near the Somme"
peTUNia! beGONia! peTUNia! peTUNia!

from field maneuvers staged in Tennessee
peTUNia! beGONia! rose-rose-rose! peTUNia! peTUNia!

from battles in the 40s near the Rhine
rose-rose-rose beGONia! BLOOM! rose-rose.

BLOOM! peTUNia!
BLOOM! BLOOM-BLOOM!

a few far-off poppies,
and in the silence, a vision of the proud
gladiolus.

2. The Senile General Contemplates a Snail

your cave lurked dim beyond my dew
air billow cases soared us aloft
glazed were the crepts our mergings knew
in the gracious daze we donned and oft

O morning stain that marked our stealth!
O wistfulness! O west cargo!
weren't we one dear innershell
on pulsing bed   one live chateau?

a taintair and believered sigh
I offer all who laugh then lapse

and you with your cold and stoning eye
I kiss in my apocalypse

3. The Senile General Remembers High School

We used to sneak away
from Virgil's dull hexameters
or Caesar's Vercingetorix and play the radio.

Sometimes brave triumvirates conspired to commit
"twin-killings," and quick historians,
Reagan, Allen, trochaic and hysterical,
extolled the deed the moment it took place.

Now although the sponge of memory cakes inside
my brain, I can still recite by heart
the old heroic catalogue,
mono-syllabic and vernacular:

Zack Wheat Ty Cobb Clint Frank Ken Strong
Mel Ott Chuck Klein King Carl Prince Hal
BABE RUTH (Ah, The Babe! Cheez, The Babe!)

Brief potent sounds, like "God," like "Christ,"
partanomastically profound:
Ken (mind), *Strong* (body),
Babe (Messiah), *Ruth* (mercy).

Almost all forgotten now (Not Ruth! Not Ruth!)
impalpable and dumb (Not Ruth!)
in some celestial stadium
where two exhausted teams
are playing, still, the first game ever played
and God is in the stands.

4. McCaffery's Solitaire (Nurse's notes)

from 1 P.M. to 2:15 he played
a kind of solitaire with six or so
uncertain photographs
he thumbed them down with care

complained about a missing
ACE
was told to wait

complained he could not see their
EYES
was told to look again

played a round of "faces wild"
complained about a missing
SPADE
was told to wait

complained about a missing
CHUCK
was told the chuck was there

exclaimed he was about to
CHEAT
was told to go ahead

complained about a missing
CHILD
was told the child was there

at 2:15 began to whimper
asked for different cards

5. Transfusions

Nourished through a needle, waiting for the nurse,
I sleep.
Somewhere back there, inside my dream, beyond my room,
ancestors converge,
a nameless multitude engaged in random copulation,
myriad couples coupling
whose every throbbing heart throbs on in mine.

Set on the stretcher
I think of tables bearing flesh for holidays,
sliced and scraped from bone,
with other flavors out of seed, vine, branch, earth,
ploughed for, bedded, plucked, picked,
gathered on the table,
swallowed into further flesh, and seed, and blood.

Trundled toward the operating room,
I contemplate again the history of my blood
pulsing down the centuries,
closer at last than history,
coursing through the heat and verve of recent hearts:
   Hank and Emma   Lizzie and Chips
      Henry and Edna-clair

      ***   ***   ***

Every holiday with nursing care
my mother, Edna-clair,
would baste the dinner turkey,
sleek belly browning in the stove,
warm as a womb,
succulent paunch ready to be carved . . .

I drowse off into surgery.

6. McCaffery's Bardo

(Bardo: a dreamlike state between life and death, influenced by the spiritual support of attendent relatives and friends.)

He wasn't quite anonymous in air. Pain
surged through caverns in his skull,
but he was almost loose above his bones.

Sister Thomasine sat down beside his bed,
chaste and in her twenties once again,
concerned about his conscience and his death

now, in penultimate Miami, even now.
She called him firmly by his Christian name,
and once again she led him by the hand
where incense burned near marble long ago,
past faces in the stations of the cross
toward the wistful gaze of a one-eyed pastor.

But pain blanked through his skull down there.
He shuddered, hovering above the wrinkled nun,
who called him shrilly by his family name
while he flew far beyond her angry voice
to find behind the bounds of Paradise
the truant pastures of eternity,
nameless as Miami to a bird.

7. McCaffery's Karma

I lapsed from drying daylight down
through slippery dreams and jellies of old memories
toward another womb

      soul-in-soul again

I bathe toward waking, sweet moist waiting.

The Final Flight

The final flight was quite uncertain.
I accounted for the shift of shadow
because the window curtain
that kept dusk solemn in the meadow
shivered from the sill;
I saw the meadow. It was still.

I had been certain that with human death
there is, invisibly, the final flight,
swift with the anguish of the latest breath
and birds shriek wildly in the night.
I was one to watch him die.
These legends lie.

The little flame above the candle glittered
evenly. I thought it best to leave.
There reached us muffled through the curtain
the common song a late bird uttered
wild with life and very brief.
The final flight is quite uncertain.

All One Breath

Thomas Kelly

Fourth Commandment

They started as giants huge and loving.

They diminished imperceptibly.
From the bedroom I heard the two of them
squabbling in the living-room.

I held onto beds and table-legs and chairs.
I learned to walk.

Hunting & gathering, my Father found
scudding on the pavement
a twenty-dollar bill.

8,000 Gum-Drops! 200 Loaves! 10 bottles of Gin!

A sporty God revealed himself
in the midst of depression.

I learned to pray.

In the time of hunger   Hitler   Hoover
God revealed himself.

By the time my father died
I was just his size.

***   ***   ***

In sleep sometimes I try
to force them to apologize:

Father! you forgot to say thank you!
You left the table, the room, the world,
without excusing yourself!

Mother! Have you done your homework?
Never talk with your mouth full!
Keep covered; *it's cold out.*

Mom! Dad! Don't talk back to me!
Never ever talk back!
Never! Never! Ever!

All right! All right! You're grounded!
Just for that you're grounded!
How about THAT! Grounded forever!
Don't tell ME that's not fair!

Just wait till I'm your age Just you wait
You'll see . . . You'll see . . .

Early Mission

I fly the Gotha past my bed,
soar above the reading lamp, and swoop
down toward the rocking-chair.

Looked upon from flight,
the shaggy rug tilts left, tilts right.
The surface of the floor lies flat
but violence seethes beneath
in the parlor just below.

The family's fighting there,
Central Powers, *Entente Cordial*,
fighting in the kitchen, in the parlor,
fighting everywhere,
Passchendaele, Armentieres, everywhere.

I dove down toward the table,
moderate reddish, well-scratched brown mahogany,
a target worth at least one bomb.
Down below the fighting rages on.
In the heat of battle someone shouts my name;
I drop the plane.

Sniper

I draw a bead on Daddy's Nash.
K-CHOW!
I missed.
K-CHOW! Wounded him.
K-CHOW! K-CHOW!

DEAD!

Daddy, ignorant survivor, waves,
parks the car
and waves again.

Beyond Victory

> "What did you get those medals for?"
> "For killing a lot of guys."
>
> —From *Beyond Victory*

I don't recall the movie, now,
but I recall the dream that night.
I watched myself, wounded and about to scream,
my family in another room, my Captain dead;
blood-stains spoiled my Christmas soldier-suit.

I saw me spewing luke-warm cream of wheat
on soggy lumps of mud in no-man's-land.
Face on the pillow, I heard me cry
for strong grown-ups to come and rescue me,
and scold the frightened soldiers on both sides.

Dawn rose upon a field of shining headstones,
spaced, rank and file, on gleaming blades of grass.
An eighty year old priest was celebrating mass.
My waking silenced him.

Puberty

FIRE TWO! I pulled the lanyard
one year after I couldn't learn the Lindy-Hop at
BLAM!
the Friday-Night-Confraternity-of-the-Christian-
Doctrine Dance
FIRE TWO!
Underneath the dresses and the lingerie,
the flesh bloomed lush and sacred,
full of grace.
BLAM!

Hundreds of fingers jerked the lanyards,
long hot muzzles blast-off, blast-off,
blast-off, all over Europe.

Fire-mission, counter-battery done,
I shouted into space gone all but still,
"Was it good for you?"
thinking somewhere shameless blondes
lie prone and bleeding.

In a slit-trench dream
elegant skeletons danced in my skull,
flirting, despite their lost pudenda.
No flesh, no blood. Bone on bone,
they clicked and clattered all sleep long.

First Will and Testament

[as required by Army regulations for those entering combat]

I, Corporal Kelly,
sound of mind, sound of body,
[*mens sana in corpore sana*]
one year after freshman-fall-semester, SJU,
[*vox clamantis in deserto*]
this Sixth of April, 1942,
bequeath:

To my Mother
a fistful of untolled rosary beads
and the notion that I still believe
[*Nate, quis indomitas tantus dolor excitat iras?*]

To my Father
the meaning of our muscles, flexed or limp.
Near-sighted now, he nods like Homer,
tries to remember the First World War
[*Dulce et decorum . . . etc.*].

To the girl from whom I copied High-School Latin
and with whom I almost learned to love
[*puella? femina? Mulier?*]
I leave a cold and posthumous moon.

Note. Line 11: "Son, what great pain rouses thy indomitable rage?"
Aeneid, Bk. II, 594.

Tom Kelly's Journal: Two Kills

[Jersey City, 1928]
Battles I fought in bed as a boy
roared me to sleep.
I, the perfect shot, slaughtered Turks and Germans,
almost every night, ignored wounds,
fought on until I fell.

***   ***   ***

[Les Vosges, October '44]
Maternal, non-combatant, doomed,
the first dead I ever saw,
a cow-corpse on its side,
front leg fragile, taut,
pointing at us: *THEY* did it, *THEY*
did it.

Irrelevant fatality. I pictured steak
and milk and quiet pastures.

A man with nothing else to do
could snap the leg off,
and hear the bloodless crack.

We left her there still pointing,
"*Sieg Heil!*" Sgt. Gillyard said.
"a vegetarian like her *Feuhrer*"

***   ***   ***

[Black Forest, April '45]
A perfect shot; above the eyes,
below the helmet and the hair.
Twelve years old. Slightly more?

Above the blood his hair was blond,
The uniform was not his size.
I turned away, stalking grown-ups.

Entreaty ['45]

Through the window I heard
twelve golden children lilt my pseudonym,
"Erich Von StROheim." My phoney name
offered them the afternoon before:

"Vie heisen zie?" "Erich Von Stroheim, *kinder*."
"Erich Von Stroheim?" "*Ja*."

"Erich Von StROheim . . . Eric Von StROheim . . ."
I, Erich Von Stroheim, AKA Cpl. Kelly, USA,
would I, a funny friendly guy, almost twenty-five,
wake up, get out of bed, come down and play?
Go down and play? I? Harold Ely, play?

I don't know. What would the grown-ups say?

Nostalgia Bar

for Mike Starrs

> *Nothing plaintive, nothing sad,*
> *Nothing but the gay,*
> *Lift the little glass*
> *That we might greet the day*
>   —an Old-Child's Song

Some nights:
we played with High-School Latin:
"*Hic Haec Hokum . . .*"
Caesar died with a swollen vocative:
Et TU?

Some nights:
I told tail-gunner tales, part fable and part farce:
"The target duly bombed, I counted stars
and raised my tenor voice
above the bomber's baritone,
all the way back to base."

Some nights
I sit and drink alone.

One night
there wasn't too much moon,
I started counting stars again,
golden, numberless, in the wide black cold.
Their heartless light, older far than Rome,
shone down upon the brief, surviving bunch of us.

Valor

                    In childhood
and through most of puberty, I dreamed
I would be brave in the proud smoke of battle
and loved by healthy girls whose flesh I'd spare
by wounding other flesh

                    and I believed
whatever weapon pierced my flesh,
bullet, shrapnel, sword, or bayonet, renewed
the sacred penetrations that sanctify the world:

            Adam in Paradise
            Cain at the plow
            Mary and her Ghost
            the nails that pinioned Christ

But once in war I came to know
I was outranked by any child
great moonlight bombers slew

PROFESSOR KELLY

. . . the mind arises as a result of physical
interactions . . . ranging from the
molecular to the social.

—Gerard M. Edelman

Invocation

Sing, heavenly Moose! Make thou the depth
of swollen midnight darkness risible.
I pine for paronomastic brilliancies
provoking laughter preternatural,
monstrous undulations of giggle and guffaw
as though old Aeolus and some companion gods
of flatulence and storm send gasps
and gusts of wind that, gathering, explode
in ruthless hurricane across the lawns
of Troy, and Rome, and Gloversville, New York.
O Horned God of Comedy, I beg
the balm of wide approval and applause.

A Letter from Tom Kelly, Sr.

My breath fogs a bit of windowpane
as I look out, half-hoping you'll be there,
walking up the lane,
staring at the house, staring at the door.

You always stared ahead to where you meant to get:
out of the crib, out of the bed,
out to the weatherside of the windowpane.

Now you stare through new vicinities
in their exciting climate, I suppose;
strange and novel landscapes
provocative and beckoning
beyond the reach of my old love,
my weathered voice.

I shout against the wall sometimes
toward where I think you may have gone.

I see a sphere
bright on the trunk where the heavy branch had been.
Time has healed it to a kind of crust;
I think it was the wind that wiped it smooth and clean.
But the branch is gone.

Huddling here in base-board heat
I feel the cold;
despite the thermostat
I feel the cold,

A private winter's working
in my bones, and in my blood.

I stare against the weather of my memory,
feeling cold.

Snorkeling

> . . . but the fear exists,
> *Delenda est Carthago* on the rose horizon
> —Derek Walcott

I, too, scan the bottom, tracing old
embattled landscapes, and, yes, among them
Cato's Africa, revived in High-School Latin,
and among them even old Manhattan,
long before it found its "iron ground."

But I'd rather watch the fish.
From time to time they play like schoolmates
flashing as they try to learn
the wordless syntax of their shallows.
Through every surge of current, every turn
of tide, their "time" is simply now.

Or so I've come to think, as I,
an aging Yankee in a young and wealthy country,
repeat the pompous "passive periphrastic,"
Delenda est Carthago. Well, I suppose
history threatens each *Carthago*,
call it Rome, Jerusalem, Baghdad, or Chicago,

even as I float above the fish, a chubby God,
soft and horizontal, belly slightly scarred,
watching plunge and pivot, dance and dart.

The Rat

Walking down the cemetery road
I came upon the body of a rat
spared by scavengers, apparently intact
in open air beside the buried dead.

Prosperous paunch,
a silent bulge against the tarmac black,
its blacker tail
tapered toward the roadside trench.

I hate rats. Shrewd, they scrounge through filth
and prosper, giggling, squealing, nibbling,
in ghetto walls, or barns, or scuttling
through fetid fields of death.

Not this one, for a moment, not this one
still soft to sight. I saw its corpse
like someone slain you trip across,
enemy or friend, after battle's done,

field-rations clumped in the dead crop,
stiffening away like any mortal man,
like any guy, every lust, every hope,
every instinct, gone.

Kelly and Some Graves

St. Moling built a little church called
"Templenaboe." In former times
unbaptized children were buried there.

In St. Moling's grave-yard   Kelly spied
three small globes,
each with a crucifix inside:

A dead white Y   on a bright black cross,
luke-warm liquid   shining glass.

He stole the globe on the farthest left,
Patron Ghost   of the damned and lost,
who'd bad-mouthed Christ   and paid the cost.

He brought the Thief   to Templenaboe
placed the globe   above children's bones
under weeds,   dead branches,   wordless stones,
who wait for the   Apocalypse
and nowhere to go.

Obese as Buddha

> *Poets, remember your skeleton. In youth*
> *or dotage remain as light as ashes.*
>
> —Kay Boyle

Obese as Buddha, I betray my bones,
slim and burdened under bulge and bulge of flesh,
a living, obscene burial.

Poet with tenure, I snorkel on sabbatical,
a plump and pompous blimp over swift
and slender fish; never far from shore and sandwiches.

A social square, a bloated sphere,
a pudding paradox, I would appear
narrow and rectangular.

Despite the glee of gluttony, I want to be
proud as Freud, zensitive as Kerouac,
with the sleek libido of a shark.

Interrogating the Ph.D.-Proposal

Demythdefying, defable-izing,
every yarn of barn or bastion
choralled in the old abandoned pastures:
there won't be, were not, are not
few sure pastorals in our presence
every monetary bee swarms away
and the flies of textures are upon U
wend a re-dun-dance of engine histree
scents all the tragic eros
rolling prone and supineless tunhill
to hades and gentle-sex off one and dozing off tether
obfuscating on thin I's
with the high source writerless and none
to read a read a meter made
but the might misty-flying epic Theorist
putses best footnote forward in hirs post-ductoral feces
the purplish or pear-ish apple source, the vestigial appendix
afall human history
from the snack in desanctifying grass
Till the study of the study of the study of
the last lost problemicised and blasted
inturdeggschewall canonicity.

Puntheism

> I gag on jargon, but it pays my way;
> it is deeply creative to exploit a cliché
>
> —Dr. Sigmund Jung

Lacan is up to his old catoptrics;
furthermore, his is a false image in his own Lacan-glass.
My ex-therapist is non-directive and Lacanic.
She told me I am not the only one to pun on nuns,
but to dream nun-puns is idiopathic.
Almost every night nuns tell me to eschew gum.
I tell them I never eschew anything I can swallow.
They tell me to stop punning about them.
I assure them I'll kick the habit.
They remind me that pious ejaculations,
that is to say, intense little prayers,
help prevent sins of emission.
And whenever I feel like sinning
I should ask the Blessed Virgin to help me.

My counselor informed me that Lacan makes all this clear.
"The diagnosis is simple:
You are muddle-aged;
Your nunnage is complicating your dotage;
therefore,
since you have a debt-wish, keep a budget
and respect the treasure principle.
You want to deride Derrida. DON'T!
Take comfort in Lacan's maxim:
'We see ourselves in a glass starkly.'
After a few more sessions you won't need to pun;
you won't have nun problems at all.
Remember,
puns are the lowest farm of humus;
Puns are dishonest, totally fraudulent!"

Lacanagain

Mendacious as mirrors, as memory.
image on a red-brick wall
image in the wind
the piss in epistemology.
the sip in insipid.
lacan with the wind.

About Lower Case

he sent his talk-poem toward the capitals of the earth
         preaching the cult of lower case
and except for inverted commas all his punctuation
         was
                  space

once or twice he seemed to think it nice
to *italicize* and i guess i find it
negatively grand that he never used the ampersand
well in one talk-poem at least

i kinda guess that i m the kinda guy
who likes to leave every bit of lint unpicked
and every hair unsplit ask my barber ask my tailor
but i note that someone adorned a talk-poem title
with a coupla caps like this

"Radical Coherency"

and after the final lyrical lower-case verse
there hangs a little asterisk

i suppose or maybe i kinda guess nobody *speaks* in up-
or low-er case but i cant tell by listening
whether commas are more like time than space

but i believe in immanent, not transcendent, meditation
and *t*-m but *i*-m
and only a liberal- dilettante- anarchist would let them
place an asterisk
after a talk-poem and cap the title

but i think hes gonna collect all unused
capitals and commas and semicolons and apostrophes and periods
and save the earth and a lotta other things because

hes a regular kinda poet slightly outta kerouack
an unpedantic sorta writer who thinks of himself
as a kinda reader who makes each talk-poem
as vatic as jerry meyer long ago

Tom Kelly Mimics R-b-rts-n D-v—s

See here—I might qualify
as an artist, poet, gleeman,
mightn't I?
Something of your intellectual?
Well, possibly? Well?

And *I*
find not the slightest difficulty
in Christianity
its beauty, and its mystery.

Mary's conception was and is immaculate?
Why not?
Dry and clean and true
as your Hemingway might say?
Why not?

Macula non est in te
Catholic children sing those words
Macula non est in te
Listen to them. Listen.
Macula non est in te
For Heaven's sake,
Why not? See here,
Why not? Eh?

Museum

The figures have no significance as individuals, only elements in form and colour. The red and white of the woman accentuate the depth of the archway . . . long since vanished.
—Hermine van Guldener, *Rijksmuseum* Amsterdam Paintings

. . . long-since vanished:
that woman, red-and-white. Mrs Siess, perhaps,
who lived, I think, across the street;
long since vanished, no significance at all.

My memory's gone all sepia.
I recall her days in blurs of dull nostalgia
set in late December, early March,
"only elements of form and colour
dissolving in the hazy atmosphere."

I remember something more of Mrs Siess:
her daughter said she lost her place
in a chapter that approached despair
before the happy-ending in God's grace.
Almost there, she lost her place.

Her daughter said her heart-beat simply stopped.
At the age of fifty-eight
in the middle of a night
and the middle of a book she never finished
her heart-beat simply stopped.
Something invisible had vanished:
"Self," her daughter said; "or Soul,"
had abandoned what lay thoughtless on the bed.

I think I can compose the room:
The book lay open on her chest;
by her bed the reading lamp still shone
upon her Savior, gazing from the wall,
his Burning Heart a fist-sized candle in his breast.

Neither gaze nor candle fluttered as she died.
With dawn the lamp-light barely reached the wall
and Christ, his Heart still burning,
stared across the room
where nothing moved except the clock.

Construing *Aliquis*

I don't care about her, never did.
In Latin 4 we were assigned to give
an English version of her flaming suicide
as she cursed Aeneas, false and fugitive.

I got an A for that. To celebrate
I ordered shish-ka-bob and chomped it down
with a glass or two of coke. But
of all the words I struggled with, just one

worked long enough, worked north and west enough
to vex me even now. I can't construe the word,
can't match it with the fury of her love
(Brother Victor didn't "do" the word).

Helpless, broken-hearted, there it lies:
Someone, Something, Anyone, arise.

Never Say Dido

I look for rum in Rome,
a warm café for those like me
who know a song or two.

Taberna est in oppidum, oppidum.
There! Hear that!
There is a tavern in the town.
I ask to join. "You pass,"
they said. "You pass."
I carouse with Latin Regents!
I! Ego! I!

    She enters the café:
every breath of old-space changed.
Her scornful eyes are aimed
at every one, at anyone, at me.
I translate into schoolboy prose
the torment of this jilted Queen,
ruthless and unsatisfied.

Let there be no love
let them fight, and their children fight
and the children of their children's children

My words drone on the page, boring and grammatical;
but the Regents say I pass.

Rest Energy and the Doe

All matter possesses enormous "rest-energy."
—Nigel Calder, *Einstein's Universe*

From somewhere in the upper woods
a single burst
pierced the dark around my house
and woke some nervous dogs
and me.

Next day my summer world held calm enough,
clear, composed, and nearly motionless;
but (if I believed a book I didn't understand)
charged with its own dumb energy.
Angry implications in ordinary space.

In *that* stillness, *I* held still,
gazing from the porch through quiet light,
down along the sloping lawn
to the shaded company of trees
a stride or two beyond
the shiny surface of the pond.

The doe intruded gently from the copse
at the bottom of the lawn;
there followed one, and then another, fawn
thirsty, hungry, irresponsible.
Now and then I seemed to sense her scold
as she watched them splash and sip and nibble.
Loving them, she listened to the silence
in the potent world surrounding them,
ready for whatever might be lurking there,
like me.

They passed quite near the porch.
She stopped and briefly contemplated me.
I thought I saw resentment in her eyes
before she turned away and led them off
toward the upper woods where everything,
just then, seemed still.

About His Grandson

He runs ahead of me. I call him back.
"Stay near me, Steve, until we reach the park."
He no longer toddles, loves to run
until he's out of breath. "Stay near me, Steve,
it's almost, almost dark."

I'd like to tell him "Paradise" means "walled-in park"
where no one ever had to feel ashamed
and none were ever old enough to totter,
and beauty was not yet sin-deep,
and none would sense a pun in "out-of-breath."
Long before the apple and the snake,
long before the scepter and the orb.

He runs ahead of me toward years and days
and afternoons I'll never know. Even so
I try to call him back. Even so,
call him back and stay forever
in the daylight in the park.

Pneumatics

Pneuma: *breath, spirit, soul,*
that which is blown or breathed.

Something flows away.
Not like the luke-warm breath
in old balloons we played with once.
Small quick bursts that made me cry.
And quite unlike the hiss of air
when they fluttered, crazy, through the room,
striking wall and bed and chair,
sagging down at last
limp and flaccid on the floor.

I think of death sometimes when I think
of flight. Sometimes . . .
Once near summer's end I watched a bird
clearly dancing to her own delight,
a solo turn beyond all words, all jargon,
no "thermal currents," only shining summer air,
sheer joy, high glee, and wild control.

Whatever broke her dance I can't explain.
Her music changed, perhaps, or stopped.
I heard no shot,
but what took place was quick,
a drop of breathless weight,
an empty lump that briefly shocked
the flowing branches of a willow tree.

Convalescent

I left the ward "barely fixed,"
Scotch-tape safety-pins a little glue,
staples and a tack or two,
my bones so many twigs and sticks.

The maples had shed for winter,
December skeletons, freezing on the lawn
in cold clean space.

As late as August, juicy green,
they'd sparkled through the pane,
before the symptoms, red and brown,
glowed on dying leaves.

So, at least, lying in the bedroom,

I remembered them, as I seemed to feel
soul and mind and memory,
all one transparence, easing toward
a fine and final otherness,
all-encompassing, voluptuous.

I heard words they'd made me memorize
years and years before: "All one breath."
The beasts and I, and the birds that fled the cold
while leaves were letting go:
"All one breath."

A Sermon Kelly Never Heard

Cecidit de coelo stella parva
—distorted from *Revelation*

A small star falls, still shining.

Now Listen!
In the beginning will be the Word
Genesis succeeds Apocalypse;
God anticipates what happens long ago,
as Ecclesiastes says.

The small star shines forever, falls again, shines on;
the breath of God still moves upon the waters.

Meantime you Faithful dip your hand
in luke-warm water,
to bless yourselves.

Do it as you think of death
and clock-time ticking
toward contradictions of eternity

when once again you'll wait
in the starless space before your birth.

Waiting for Beckett

He was having us on. What he was doing
was having us
on.
Had us on
and now he's gone
like THAT.

Space shrank toward him. That's what happened.
Space
narrowed to nothing.
The old horizon closed inside
the unsurrounding center of the world.
Center swallowed circumference.
That's what happened;
scape lost scope:

World-scape, sky-scape, sea-scape,
land-scape, room-scape, skull-scape,
ZERO.

There's no *here* here
now that he's gone there.
There? Gone there? Where?
We don't know where. Anywhere.
So there!

Nothing itself happens there.
There is where nothing is itself.

vale atque ave

Something here, then? Listen . . .

Something? Here?

Having us on?

Listen . . .

Coma

for Tom Kelly, Prof. Emeritus

I

I touched your brow and wondered . . .
a conscious nothing darkening?
Another pun for me that never quite escaped?
Unlikely fragments out of Tao:
"deep . . . it's darkly visible . . . it only seems . . ."?

***   ***   ***

I'll flee the final stitch of time
and fly through vehement winds
past the geese of the kingdom
beyond the farthest rim of space

Bright stars stare inside my dream until
dawn works grey in the haze of my head
gleaning through synaptic guesspells:

Matthew-Mark-Luke-and-Warm:
this is *the scene where I came in,*
when all is sad in dawn.
I'll shuffle off this mortal soil.

II

Was there a kind of etymon in matter
and we, so many names, its progeny?
An utterance before sound,
no word yet possible,
and SHE was there, the Etymom?

Precursor molecules spawned us;
progeny through energy in rock,
ancestors, pre-syllabic, pre-subjective,
dumb but fecund? Atom then Eve?

. . . Eve and, lighter than air,
the human mind
(attitude and craft):

slabs and lintels, Stonehenge,
Attic ruins in forgotten sunlight
(bright broken beauty, shining still)

the few teeth left in a pauper's mouth,
dentures in my Father's water-glass,
sleek shapes of steel, soaring, sensing,
shattering,

and the mushy tangled brain inside my skull,
about to dry away and suffocate
the memory of Molly Kule,
the Mother of us all.

Waking Towards the Last December

Nomads Land! Sguarll and squeaks in the fearist.
Cant see the floress for the freeze:
     The daze of the mumps mismumbled
     as the sleaves on the breeze autumbled.
     They are misflamed, miscountered.

O, let the Viatic come.
Pop Prelatzers and whine to fry
in the lowest fright of angels.
Oh for one auGUST of wind! One ice septender tray!
The last placemeal! The lost treadmeal!
Oh, munch the whole-wheat white-attic crumb!

Drowned in deep-ocean, drained of devotion,
a weed to the wide is surf-fishing:
"In the Beckoning was the Void."

Those were his lost birds,
flown through the winter-pain of death.
He dried sceneless. All his mortal sense forsaken.
        Oh, the underscraper will scour his skin
        till the scars shine.
     His day that rose in dusk unto dusk it is interned.

Elegy for Thomas Kelly

Ah, Tom, what are metaphors but fertile lies?
You'd say "This" is "That," and hope
the loving world believed. It tries.

Precocious still in later middle-age,
a timeless *wunderkind*, you memorized
each day. Each day you learned your part,
reliving even as you lived.
Invoking old Euhemerus,
you got down every day by heart,
embellishing for retelling.

Tom, we're both still boasting in the yard
after school lets out,
Miltonic metaphors meant to readjust
the ways of God to us;
metaphors, not similes.
Valiant lies
we even bring to bed with us
to fill the time it takes to fall asleep
proud, naïve, and credulous.

Well Tom,
every "That" has come at last to "This":
We're working to preserve contending versions of your memory.
We're reaching, Tom, for every one of you.
Come home and tell us all you did or might have done,
or all we know you did not do.
Tell us now, before the night gives way
to one more ordinary day.

CAIN AND OTHER RELATIVES

Cain

Remember, Abel murdered first, killed a "creature,"
one our Father Adam named
after we were made to leave
the walled-in park where Eve,
our Mother,
shared with him the fruit of knowledge
and made us mortal.
He named us all: Tiger, Turtle, Serpent,
Lamb
named me "Creature," Abel "Son,"
every creature named, every single one;
but none was slain until
Abel offered God his kill
and God approved.

I never fatted calf or lamb for sacrifice.
I, named "Creature," knew each beast
even as I knew myself.
I offered bread and wine,
crust and juice, nothing in disguise,
no hidden clots or scars.
My apples stored no guilt.

Among His avatars, I venerated Ceres, hated Mars.
I consecrated bloodless feasts
to celebrate the harvest, sang "Te Deum Laudamus"
and left each lamb of God feeding in the field.

I Slew Abel

and it came to pass that the Lord destroyed every
living substance, "both man, and cattle,
and the creeping things,
and the fowl of the heavens,
and they were destroyed from the earth
and Noah only remained alive."

I slew Abel
And it came to pass that Abraham meant to slay Isaac
and the Lord said, "because thou hast not withheld thy son,
thine only son,
I will bless thee."

I slew Abel
And it came to pass that the Psalmist sang,
"Happy shall he be that taketh and dasheth
the little ones against the stones."

Two Meals

And it came to pass:
> Chips Kelly waked to the rage of whirling birds
> screeching near his window;
> saw the sparrow-hawk stun a fledgling rook
> rise & strike again,
> hold the vague-eyed creature down, clutched in claw,
> bite through feathers, bite through skin,
> wrench off gobs of flesh,

skirr off, slaked and buoyant.
skinny skeleton and skull
useless in the fading rage.

> Chips scrambled eggs for breakfast.

Cute Kelly's Semi-Final

Chips hears a housefly thud against the pane
a bit above a spider web,
buzz back and turn and hit again
and lumber off in shock,
perplexed by hard transparencies,
sophisticated space.

> Chips remember Cute, his brother, jabbed and jabbing,
> red gloves smashing swollen flesh,
> blood across his eye;
>
> lost six straight and quit for good
> mumbled into waves of buzzing space,
> a puzzled yearning in his gaze.

The fly writhes, fighting in the web;
Chips squashes it against the sill,
more to spare the little jerk than kill.

Dennis (Chips) Kelly on Pension

Sleeping in his rocker, Chips walks his beat,
glazed streets in gaslight
littered with thugs and thieves;
bastards, murderous bastards, battered and prone.
Chips blows the whistle, clubs the curb,
waits for the Lads to come
and cart the garbage off. He waits alone.

The rocker creaks;
lips pursed, he stirs, fist clenched and empty.
Whatever that was, it was not the Lads.
Eyeing a sinister window,
he blows the whistle, clubs the curb again.

Down the street a rag-time slut
hears the noise and strolls away.
He waits alone.

Where are the Lads?
The rocker creaks
and wakes him to the room,
quiet, blurred, and warm.
He sees the glossy windowpane
this side of everybody else's night.
Where are the Lads?
Nobody heeds him anymore.

Patchy Pete, the one-eyed cat,
prowls the alley, snarling and secure.

Uncle Gus Kelly

1. Spring 1938

Toward the very last, almost dead,
Gus Kelly,
[Baseball-fan, Salesman, Poker-man, *St. John's Alumnus*] said,

"The cards God dealt were low,
mostly spades, none really wild,
and none of them, none of them, a joker.

"I had," he said, "a paradox for openers, and a rare
deck of baseball cards for sentimental solitaire
when nobody else, nobody else, nobody else was there.
Not Zeke Bonura, not Bordagoray, not
'Boots' Poffengerger, not 'Blubber' Malone.
I was alone.

"Not Hal Schumacher, 17,
not Mel Ott, (number 3? Number 8?)
I watched *those* two play a nearly perfect game.
They were great. They were great
(cheap bleacher-seat for maybe half-a-buck
in Ebbest Field in '38. In 1938.).

" 'Schumie' shut them out; and Mel Ott shot
a big one into Bedford for the only score.
And Rosen, Goody Rosen, got . . . Rosen got?
. . . the only Dodger hit.

"He was erased at second base.
I don't recall his number; I don't recall his face,
but he was erased, all right,

at second base, a double-play,
'twin-killing' they sometimes say.
Oh, he was erased!

"I ran across their names again
in Zinnser's history course:
Eugene Ott, who served the Reich,
a general, a diplomat.
And a Shumacher named Kurt,
who lost a leg
from torture in a concentration camp.
A Socialist, Zinnser sneered. A Social Democrat.

"For all I know,
there might have been a Jew named Rosen, squeezed
inside a box-car with a number on his arm;
more digits than on Goody's uniform.

"On the day I watched the game
I'd never heard of them.
I was a fan; I watched the game.

"As for history: I suppose
The Brooklyn Eagle's 'Morgue' has Goody's name
somewhere in a box-score.

"Nowadays they mostly play at night;
but the lights are going out
and I forget the score,
or maybe I don't care.
And nobody else is there; just me alone.
Nobody else is there.
And maybe I don't care."

2. Nuncs

Time is a succession of nuncs
                            –Aquinas, perhaps.

I'm running out of nuncs. Running out.
They were beautiful,   a few of them;

Some guys had a basket-full, some a box,
some a little paper bag,
and one of them a handful in his pocket;
I forget his name.
Father Brood said he'd save them for his coffin
and for the after-life
where there's a lot of them,
a Jacob's pot of them.

What do they look like? Nuncs?
They're transparent. Brief. They're infinitesimal . . .
They leave on arrival.

UNCLE ORVILLE AND BEATRICE

Liturgy: Father, Fowl, and Daughter

> *In general, flying signifies transformation*
> *from a worse state to a better, and hence*
> *renewal and rebirth.*
>
> —C. G. Jung

Orville Ely,
assiduous and apron-clad, bastes with seasoned sauce
a tender chicken, slain and smoldering on the coals.
He favors recipes from Zosimus
or any ancient alchemist
whose cooking methods Jung preserved for us:

> *Take a fowl [volatile]*
> *cut off its head with a fiery sword*
> *pluck out its feathers, then separate*
> *its limbs and cook it slow*
> *over a charcoal fire till the bird*
> *burns down at last to a single shade.*

His guests and family gather on the lawn,
eager to swallow the sacrifice
and praise the host, partly to atone
with him who sweats a bit
over blood and body, spice and sauce,
brooding till the crackling sizzles down.

Atone? At one
in the afternoon?
With whom? With him? With Ely?

> *. . . a fair-haired man with dark-blue eyes*
> *immersed in a jar of sesame oil*
> *was fed with figs for forty days . . .*
> *they tore off his head and packed it round*
> *with cotton wool and placed it on*
> *burnt olive-ash. Its eyes could see*
> *but the lids could not move,*
> *it revealed to the people their inmost thought.*

Sipping from his glass at last,
he sees his daughter Beatrice munch a wing
and watch a turkey-vulture hunger through the air.

> *. . . in order to renew the moon-goddess*
> *a maiden was decapitated, skinned;*
> *a youth then put the skin around him*
> *to represent the goddess, risen once again.*

Bird and girl adorn the afternoon.
As Orville stares the vulture out of sight,
some words of Bryant touch his "inmost thought":
. . . abyss of heaven . . . swallowed up thy form.
He shifts his stare to Beatrice and her grin;
this time she wants a leg, without the skin.

Note. Quotations from C. G. Jung, "Transformation Symbolism in the Mass," *Papers from the Eranos Yearbooks*, Vol. II.

Principal Parts: Orville Ely

Day in day out, night after night,
School-Superintendent Ely searched for Bea, little Bea,
even for the Bea that ran away, sulked off,
bad grammar, new nobility, cheap,
sulked off, in a rage of raucous music
after the last retarded tantrum,

from a home where
he could bathe himself clean as his grammar
where the soap smelled moral
the porcelain looked Protestant;
linen and shirt and soul, all unstained,
he worshipped a clean-cut Christ.

Grace was said before each meal
one mistake in grammar earned an insult
two mistakes in grammar earned a slap,
three mistakes in grammar sent one from the table.
Grace was offered after every meal.

. . . Searched for months through scummy neighborhoods and
    streets
reeking like latrines
Orville Ely,
well-dressed and terrified,
assaulted by the sight of life-sized dolls,
pneumatic, in flimsy, dirty lingerie,
plump and sickening, as large as Bea,
in shops that smelled of sweat and sin and urine.

Home again beside his well-washed wife
his dream sinks inside Manhattan Harbor;
pollution stains the porcelain teeth,

the swelling eyes, the gills, the membranes,
the delicate entrails of edible fish;
pollution taints the alleyways and avenues,
contaminates the breath and lungs and brains
of pigeons, pimps, and prostitutes, and the heart of prowling Ely.
His right arm long and mean,
blemished with tattoos, he prowls,
young again, silky mean, the long arm
and the mean hand like a poison-snake,
angry fingers clutching the mean knife;
Ely aches for victims, for pimps, fags,
pigeons, johns, pneumatic dolls,
runaways, runaways, runaways,
to go, going, went, GONE,
all one victim, androgynous as zeppelins,
one infected soul sloughing off in sobs of fog,
Ely himself the wounding I,
the wounded me.

About Beatrice

1. Beatrice Remembers Her Mother

Sometimes, singing me to sleep, she sang too well
and made me cry.

She sang beyond the ceiling and the moon,
she sang me past the harmony of stars,
through old expansions of the world,
through depths of midnight, and the breadth of days.
She sang into my future where I heard,
and hear, ambiguous refrains.

She sang past mountain-clouds and castle-clouds
past blues of summer near the lake,
toward winter and the silence of our life
in empty rooms abandoned long ago
where even now she's singing me to sleep
knowing where I've gone and where I go.

2. Beatrice Trip

he tranced off into my tomorrow
leaving me here in his yesterday
I'm gonna find me a friend and borrow
money for shit and blast away
earn me a sinister A K A

Christ is rocking on the mantelpiece
struttin' his stuff in a seamless gown
rehearsing an act with a coupla thieves
gonna rock & roll all over town

the bad thief drums and the good plays fiddle
with a single & a double & a triple paradiddle

sideman satan's gonna bring me down
sideman satan's gonna bring me down

3. Beatrice: Feast of the Epiphany 1948

Asleep in the street near a People's Drugstore
dreaming of milk in a shiny white bowl
I pissed in the pants I had pissed in before
while two angry angels fought for my soul

God took on flesh (so they say) in the winter
swaddled immortal and not very old
sucking soft breasts and warm in the manger
he pissed like a human asleep in the cold

4. Beatrice: *Essence* & Accident

As a child she believed
the silent hum of God
in empty black solitude
spawned a breadth of space
exploding into history

Later priests and shrinks
tried to squeak their minds
to her
(to *her*
waking to a different trauma,
invoking puns
even as they squoke)

No one heard the car brake squeal
and screech beyond her gasp
her last silent scream of consciousness

Hum is where the heart was

5. Beatrice in Surgery

The old diminished hum,
there, down there, underneath the coma,
underneath the clip, dip, snip, snap,
there, inside the shining blood, inside
the secret hollows of memory and bone
sinking past a final resonance
sounding out toward spaceless black
surrounding history.

Frightened, I shiver back to flesh,
and vulgar harmony, the mortal synthesis
of sight and sound,
     I hear a voice
implore a mourner to rejoice:
". . . he'll shine before the glory of the Beatif . . ."

Pain wrenches through my waking guts and moves me to forgive.

6. Hic Jacet Beatrice

Beatrice gone,
Orville Ely comments to his son:

"This is the way she remembered us.
Well no, she never told *me* how she remembered us.
But the friend of the therapist to whom she told it
    explained it to my colleague who recounted to me that
'This is the way she remembered us.'

"I think my colleague (sensing through the words of the
friend
    how deeply impressed the therapist was with the way she
    remembered us), was touched.

Which is to say, my colleague and his friend and the therapist,
    were not indifferent to my daughter's memory.
I find some solace thinking about these three.

"I have no image of the face of the therapist, or his friend.
My colleague, as he talked to me, seemed to stare at his
    impression of my face.

"The therapist saw my daughter's face, although
    my colleague and his friend did not.
They were given a careful version of her words
of which I have their paraphrase.

"I try to fit the face they say the therapist said he saw
with the drifting faces I recall:
One face says 'I can shay anyshing!'
One face cries at halloween.
One face only stares.

"I try to fit the faces with the paraphrase
. . . one face only stares."

New Poems

Sister Kelly

*[Macula lutea: an area in the eye near the centre
of the retina at which visual perceptions is most acute.
(New Latin, "yellow spot.")]*

Sr. Kelly, from her final pillow,
considers the synoptic eye of God
staring through the air,
                    at the plane,
                        at the sparrow,
at the soft black fly
                    round as a raisin
                        dying on the screen.

Fading, she sees her brother's face
staring from his own last place,
thirty-seven years ago.
Through the eye of God she sees him die,
a flash of skin and olive-drab
in the yellow spot of a sniper's eye.

Waking she sees a blind black spot
drying in the early light.

Hoc Est Corpus

No drama in the dream; not yet;
I seemed to hear volcanic rumbling,
read to roar,   erupt,   and spew
ancient indignation down the mountainside.

My memory and the air around me shook
before the trruth
that, muttttering, I might admit to you,
and to myself.

And to myself,
but never to the gentle voice
that could murmur me awake
before the mountain lost control.

But then I heard again the lust of Latin
and remember fingers once ordained
to hold the tortured flesh of God transformed
for anyone to see.

The Karma of Sgt. Bruce's Grandmother (1939)

She beat on a battered acoustic guitar
vaudeville songs from the First World War
she cursed the glossy cocktail crowd
who tried to keep her from the bar.

She gobbled a bottle of Guiness's stout
and cycled off toward World War II.
She yelled, "If he calls, tell God I'm out!
but I understand what He's tryin' a do."

Sgt. Bruce: Born-Again

Thou hast also given me the necks
of my enemies that I might destroy them
that hate me.

—Psalms 18:40

thirteen hours:
mean in the clean hot air the bull's-eye glared
into Sgt. Bruce's eye

his gun spat hate
into the bright black stare

nineteen hours:
Chevrons   tattooed on each arm
three-up   two-down
one set beneath a crucifix   the other under MOM

twenty-three hours:
his last bottle of a bottle
of a bottle and . . . took off

zero hours:
aimed his cycle back to Bragg;
somewhere in the fog
between Fayetteville and God
a tire, and his soul, blew out

Eternity:
Bruce shook hands with the Macho Three,
Daddy   Bubba   and the Heavy Breather.
They gave him a grin and a gold repeater.

Clairvoyance (birthday, 1985)

. . . dozed in my chair and a blur
of a world transformed the fine dry flakes
in the empty hearth
   to snow

       not swirling
             not storming
                slow

layer upon layer
            hiding at last
               a standing-stone

in a freezing field
            somewhere
               unmarked and alone

Leaves

As leaves in autumn, so the faces of my life
fall away
nevertheless I want to hear
words in the wind
as night comes on.